## ROTHERHAM LIBRARY & INFORMATION SERVICE

This book must be returned by the date specified at the time of issue as
the DATE DUE FOR RETURN.
The loan may be extended (personally, by post, telephone or online) for
a further period if the book is not required by another reader, by quoting
the above number / author / title.

### Enquiries: 01709 336774

### www.rotherham.gov.uk/libraries

# My First Book of Baby Animals

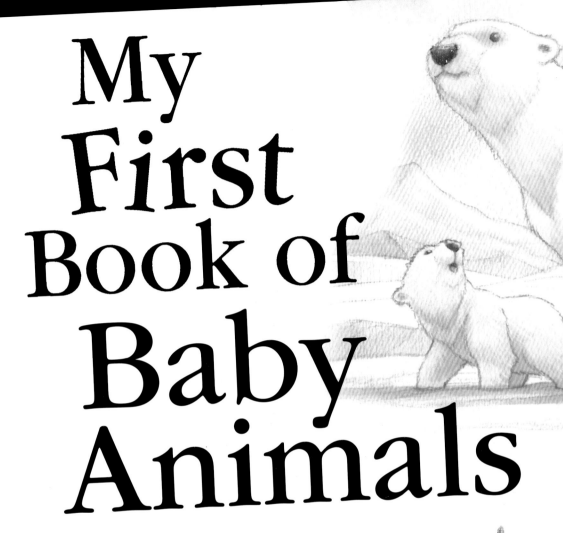

Mike Unwin

Illustrated by
Daniel Howarth

A & C BLACK
AN IMPRINT OF BLOOMSBURY
LONDON  NEW DELHI  NEW YORK  SYDNEY

# Animals growing up

Every animal starts life as a baby.

Some baby animals are born helpless, just like we are. Newborn cats can't open their eyes. They drink their mother's milk, while she keeps them safe and warm.

Other baby animals are better at looking after themselves. Baby horses can walk just a few hours after being born.

Birds hatch from eggs. Their mother does not produce milk. Their parents go out to gather food for them.

Other animals that hatch from eggs include reptiles, such as turtles. Baby reptiles look after themselves from the minute they hatch.

Are you ready to meet some baby animals?

Read the clues on each *Who is it?* page to see whether you can work out which baby animal is hiding there. Then find the answer by turning the page.

5

# How many babies?

Some kinds of animal have more babies than other kinds.
Animals with the fewest babies give them the most care.

An orangutan has just one baby at a time.

A dog may have six or more babies.

A mallard duck may have eight to twelve babies.

A green turtle may lay more than 100 eggs.
Each one contains a baby turtle.

# Who is it?

Look! Two ears are sticking out of the long grass.
And can you see those black and orange stripes?

Somebody is trying to hide.
But who is it?

# Tiger cub

It's a tiger cub. Now it's playing with its sister while their fierce mother looks on.

A tigress usually has two or three cubs. When she's away, their stripy pattern helps them to hide. It looks just like the patterns of the forest.

Playing helps tiger cubs to learn grown-up hunting skills.

8

# Who is it?

High in a tree strong little fingers
are holding on tight.

A baby animal gets a good grip
while it peeks down at the world below.

But what do you think it is?

# Baby orangutan

It's a baby orangutan. This clever little ape won't let go of its mother until it is four months old. Orangutans live in tropical rainforests. They clamber into the treetops to find ripe fruit.

A mother has just one baby every seven years. She carries it everywhere.

# Who is it?

Somebody's looking at you
with great big eyes.

Look at those lovely long eyelashes and
bright-blue tongue.

Can you guess who it is?

# Baby giraffe

It's a baby giraffe. And its mummy is standing right behind.

Giraffes are the tallest animals in the world. Their long neck helps them reach into the treetops for juicy leaves.

A baby can stand up on its long, wobbly legs as soon as it is born.

# Who is it?

Look out! Something has grabbed hold of that animal's tail.

It looks like a big, grey, wrinkly snake.

What do you think it can be?

# Baby elephant

Aha! It's not a snake but the trunk of a baby elephant.

A trunk is a special long nose. It helps elephants to touch, smell and hold onto things.

This baby elephant will soon lose its baby hair and start to grow tusks.

# Who is it?

Seen you! Two curious eyes are peeking out of the water.

Somebody is hiding in the shadow of a big rock.

Who do you think it can be?

# Baby hippo

It's a baby hippo. And that rock was really its mother. Now they have both come out of the water.

Hippos live in a group called a pod. Babies are born in the water and stick close to their mum. Her big teeth help to scare away crocodiles.

At night, mother and baby leave the river together to eat grass on land.

# Who is it?

Somebody looks warms and snug in a furry sleeping bag. Two big eyes peek at the world outside. Two pointy ears twitch at every sound.

Who do you think it can be?

# Joey

It's a baby kangaroo — also called a joey.
That sleeping bag is really a special pocket on
its mother's tummy, called a pouch.

A newborn kangaroo is no bigger than your
thumb. It stays safe inside its mother's pouch,
where it grows bigger by drinking her milk.
At six months it starts to
explore outside.

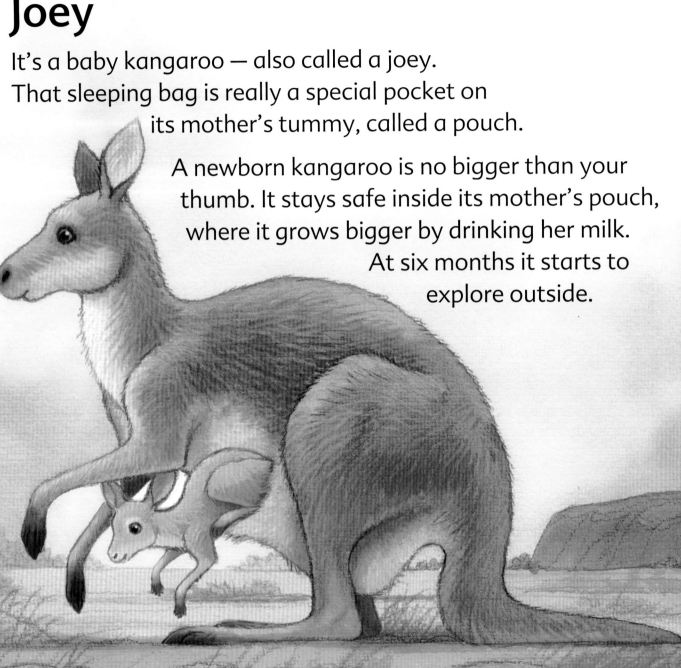

# Who is it?

These babies are taking a good look at you from inside their burrow. They think you can't see them, but you can.

What do you think they are?

# Baby meerkat

They are baby meerkats. Now they have popped outside to join their mum and look around.

Meerkats come from Africa, where they live in groups called colonies. A mother has her babies underground. One adult may babysit all the babies in the colony.

# Who is it?

Look! What's that sticking up out of the sea?

It's a big tail. And it's giving you a big wave.

But who can it be?

# Baby humpback whale

Look under the water and you can see that tail belongs to a baby humpback whale.

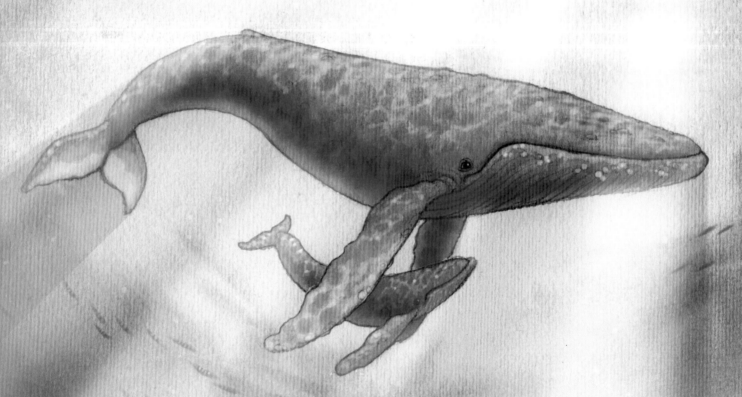

This big baby is longer than a car. But its mother is much bigger. The two stick side by side. When the mother comes up to breathe air, her baby comes up too. Together they make long journeys across the oceans.

# Who is it?

Chip, chip, chip...

Lots of eggs are buried on a sandy beach.
And it looks like one is hatching.

See that beady little eye poking out.
Who does it belong to?

# Baby green turtle

It's a baby green turtle — no bigger than your hand.

Baby turtles hatch at night and dig their way out using their flippers. Their mother is nowhere to be seen — she swam away after laying her eggs.

The beach is dangerous for baby turtles. They wriggle straight down to the sea, where they can grow up more safely.

# Who is it?

Look! Paw prints in the snow.
Somebody's been taking a walk.

It must have been somebody with great big feet to leave those great big tracks. But who do you think left the smaller tracks?

# Polar bear cub

It's a big, furry polar bear and her two little cubs.

Polar bears live in the cold Arctic. The cubs are born in a snug den beneath the snow. In spring they pop out for their first view of the world.

The mother leads her cubs down to the frozen sea. Now she must catch a seal for them to eat.

# Who is it?

Whose big bare feet are those?

And whose pointy little beak is sticking out just above them?

It looks like somebody is trying to hide. But who?

# Baby emperor penguin

It's a baby emperor penguin. And now it has popped out for a better view.

Emperor penguins live in the freezing cold Antarctic. A baby perches on its father's feet and snuggles into his tummy feathers to keep warm and cosy.

Soon its mother will return from the sea with fish for it to eat.

# Who is it?

Somebody's hiding behind a shopping bag.

Can you see that shiny wet nose and wagging tail?

Who do you think they belong to?

# Puppy

It's a puppy. And look, there are its brothers and sisters.

A female dog usually has around six puppies. Bigger types of dogs may have even more.

Puppies are born with a good sense of smell but their eyes don't open until they are ten days old. After one month they start to eat solid food.

# Who is it?

A strange creature is rolling around on the carpet!

It has two ears, paws and a tail. But it seems to be made of wool.

What do you think it is?

# Kitten

It's a kitten. And it was all tangled up.

Kittens play with anything they can chase or catch, such as this ball of wool. Best of all, they like to play with each other, pouncing and tumbling.

Playing is part of growing up for kittens. It teaches them skills they'll need for when they get older.

# Who is it?

Look closely at that creature standing in the field.
Does something seem strange?

Try counting its legs.

That's right, there are eight.
Surely something must be wrong.

# Calf

Ah! It's not one cow with eight legs but two cows with four legs each. It's a mother with a baby.

A baby cow is called a calf. It stands underneath its mother to drink milk from her udder. After one week it follows her everywhere she goes.

# Who is it?

Somebody's lying down in the hay.

Those long legs are neatly folded so their owner can take a nap.

Can you guess whose legs they are?

# Foal

It's a baby horse — called a foal. See how long its legs are now? Almost as long as its mother's.

A foal can stand up just one hour after it is born.

One day later it can gallop. At three years old it is strong enough for you to ride.

# Who is it?

Boing! Boing! Two animals are bouncing up and down in the spring sunshine.

One is black and the other is white. And both have tiny hooves.

What do you think they are?

# Lamb

Those bouncing babies are lambs. Newborn lambs stick close to their mother. After a few days they form a playful gang, leaping around, bleating loudly and having fun.

Their mothers eat lots of fresh grass. This helps them make enough milk for their fast-growing babies.

# Who is it?

What a funny face! Look at those big ears and wrinkly pink snout.

This baby animal is having a good sniff around.

But what do you think it is?

# Piglet

It's a piglet. And it has lots of brothers and sisters. Now they are all drinking milk greedily from their mother. Don't worry — she has enough to feed them all.

A female pig is called a sow. She gives birth to a litter of ten babies or more. Each one drinks so much milk that its weight doubles in just seven days.

# Who is it?

These baby birds are hiding in the dark, waiting for their parents to return.

What strange faces they have!
And what fuzzy feathers!

What do you think they are?

# Baby barn owl

They are baby barn owls.
Here comes their mother, with
a mouse for dinner. Yum, yum!

Barn owls nest inside old buildings
and tree holes. Their parents hunt all night to find enough food
for their hungry chicks. After 50 days the chicks have grown
their adult feathers and can fly away.

42

# Who is it?

Look at those fluffy little balls of feathers.
They are waddling along behind their mother
as fast as they can.

But what are they? And where is she leading them?

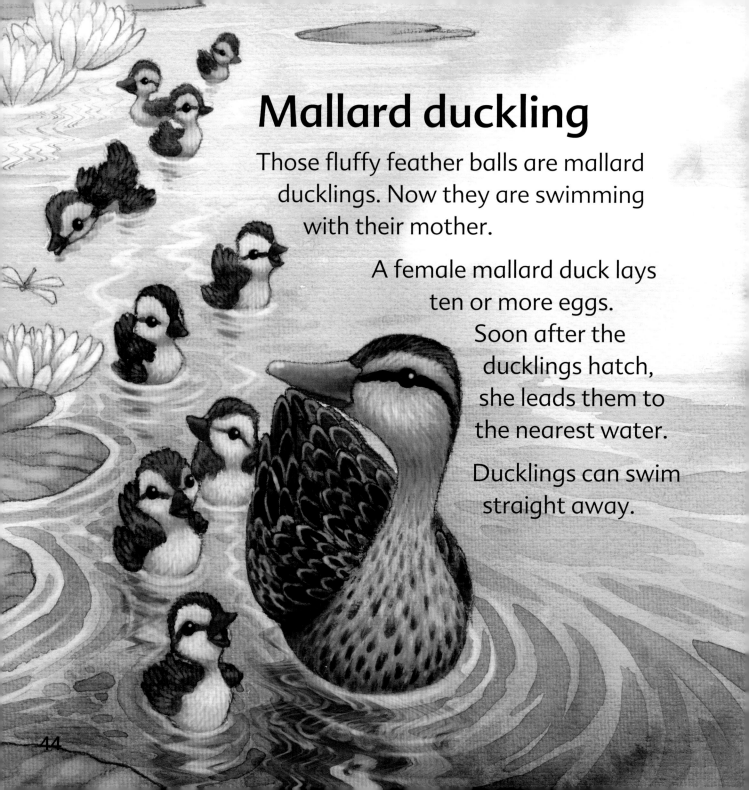

# Mallard duckling

Those fluffy feather balls are mallard ducklings. Now they are swimming with their mother.

A female mallard duck lays ten or more eggs. Soon after the ducklings hatch, she leads them to the nearest water.

Ducklings can swim straight away.

# Who is it?

Can you see those little black things wriggling in the water?

Bend down for a closer look. They've got tails, and some have got tiny legs. What are they?

# Tadpole

Those wrigglers are tadpoles. That's another name for baby frogs.

Tadpoles hatch from bubbly eggs laid in the water, called frogspawn. At first they have no legs so they swim about using their tail.

Soon they grow back legs. Then front legs. After twelve weeks, their tail disappears and they can hop about on land.

# Baby animal words

**Antarctic**  a very cold part of the world, around the South Pole.

**ape**  a type of animal, such as a gorilla, that looks like a big monkey but has no tail.

**Arctic**  a very cold part of the world, around the North Pole.

**burrow**  a hole in which an animal makes its home.

**litter**  all the babies that an animal has at one time.

**snout**  the nose of an animal.

**tropical rainforest**  thick forest in hot parts of the world where it rains all year.

# Index